$24.⁰⁰

Apple/Bond $

Smart

11-4-00

D0820805

THE
BALKANS

SIMON ADAMS

A+
Smart Apple Media

CR

NIA -
GOVIN

ERBIA
NTEN

Balkan

First published in 2004 by Franklin Watts
96 Leonard Street, London EC2A 4XD

Franklin Watts Australia
45-51 Huntley Street, Alexandria NSW 2015

This edition published under license from Franklin Watts. All rights reserved.

Copyright © 2004 Franklin Watts.

Designer: Steve Prosser, Editor: Belinda Hollyer, Art Director: Jonathan Hair, Editor-in-Chief: John C. Miles, Picture Research: Diana Morris, Map Artwork: Ian Thompson

Picture credits
AP/Topham: front cover t, front cover b,
34b, 37t
Yannis Behrakis/Reuters/Popperfoto: 35t
Bettmann/Corbis: 29tr
Terry Fincher/Express/Hulton Archive: 31t
Fotomas/Topham: 15t
Hulton/Corbis: 30b
Museum der Stadt Wien/Dagli Orti/Art Archive: 14t
Oslobodjenje Archive/Reuters/Popperfoto: 24t
Picturepoint/Topham: 13t, 25t, 29cl
José F. Poblete/Corbis: 11c
Oleg Popov/Reuters/Popperfoto: 39t
Popperfoto: 11t, 16b, 18b, 19t, 20t, 22b, 23t, 27t, 28b, 31c
Mario La Porta/Popperfoto: 32b
Rade Prelic/Reuters/Popperfoto: 38b
Hazir Reka/Reuters/Popperfoto: 41t
Hans Georg Roth/Corbis: 8b
Radu Sigheti/Reuters/Popperfoto: back cover, 33t
UPP/Topham: 36b
Nik Wheeler/Corbis: 40b

Published in the United States by Smart Apple Media
2140 Howard Drive West, North Mankato, Minnesota 56003

U.S. publication copyright © 2006 Smart Apple Media
International copyright reserved in all countries. No part of this book may be reproduced in any form without written permission from the publisher.
Printed in the United States of America

Library of Congress Cataloging-in-Publication Data

Adams, Simon, 1955-
The Balkans / by Simon Adams.
p. cm. — (Flashpoints)
Includes index.
ISBN 1-58340-603-4
1. Balkan Peninsula—History—Juvenile literature. 2. Former Yugoslav republics—History—Juvenile literature. I. Title.
II. Flashpoints (Smart Apple Media)

DR36.A3 2005
949.6—dc22   2004056456

9 8 7 6 5 4 3 2 1

CONTENTS

Introduction	**8**
Early History	**10**
Ottoman Rule	**12**
The Start of the "Eastern Question"	**14**
Redrawing the Map	**16**
The End of Ottoman Rule	**18**
World War I	**20**
The Balkans Between the Wars	**22**
World War II	**24**
The Coming of Communism	**26**
Yugoslavia and Albania	**28**
Postwar Greece	**30**
The End of Communism	**32**
The Breakup of Yugoslavia	**34**
Bosnia	**36**
Kosovo	**38**
The Balkans Today	**40**
Glossary	**42**
Index	**44**

Property of Dexter
Middle School Library

INTRODUCTION

Today, the Balkans are notorious for bitter warfare and remain one of the main flashpoints of the modern world. Yet, for most of their history, the Balkans were a fairly peaceful area. Until recently, the Balkans did not exist as a region—the name has been used for only about 100 years.

WHAT'S IN A NAME?

The region we know today as the Balkans, or the Balkan Peninsula, only acquired its name in modern times. Two thousand years ago, the region was simply part of the mighty Roman Empire. Later, it became part of the Byzantine Empire, whose capital city was Constantinople (now called Istanbul). When the Ottoman Turks conquered the area in the 15th century, they called it Rumeli: the former "Roman" lands. Its people were called Romans or just Christians. Western Europeans called the region European Turkey or "Turkey in Europe" or just the Near East.

NAMING THE REGION

The name "Balkans" was first used by the German geographer Johann August Zeune in 1808. The name was, however, based on an error. Zeune assumed that the Balkan mountains stretched right across the peninsula from the Adriatic to the Black Sea. In fact, they only run across part of Bulgaria and formed the main barrier to be crossed by European travelers going to Constantinople. But as the various peoples of the region acquired their independence from Ottoman rule between 1878 and 1913, the new name took hold. By the end of World War I, it was in common use around the world.

"The interior of the Balkan has been little explored, and but a few accurate measurements of elevation have been undertaken."

Von Tietz, a Prussian (German) diplomat visiting the region in 1833

The Balkans region is very mountainous.

THE BALKANS

The region we know today as the Balkans consists of the European part of Turkey, mainland Greece, Albania, Bulgaria, southern Romania, and the former Yugoslav countries of Macedonia, Serbia and Montenegro (including Kosovo), Bosnia-Herzegovina, and Croatia. Slovenia, once part of Yugoslavia, and Hungary are both now considered part of central Europe.

The region is very mountainous. There are few navigable rivers, and the terrain made it difficult to build good roads or canals. The first railways were only constructed in the late 1880s. Travel was often difficult. Most people lived in isolated communities not easily accessible from the rest of Europe or the Mediterranean. They often had little in common with neighbors who might live only a few valleys away.

THE BALKANS TODAY

THE PEOPLE

The people of the Balkans belong to many different nationalities and minority communities and speak numerous languages written in a variety of different scripts. Some people are Muslim; others are Orthodox, Catholic, or Jewish. Little unites them. Yet, for most of their history, they have lived together as part of one large empire after another, with no separate identities. Politically and geographically, the idea of the Balkans being made up of different peoples living in separate countries is a very recent concept.

EARLY HISTORY

The Balkans were first inhabited 200,000 years ago and were first settled around 3500 B.C. by semi-nomadic farmers from Russia. After 1000 B.C., the region fell under the control of a series of foreign empires, most notably Rome.

ROMAN RULE

During the second century B.C., the Romans began to conquer the Balkans, and they controlled the entire region by A.D. 106. They built many fine towns connected by a good road system and were the first to unify the Balkans. They gave its people a common language, Latin, although Greek was also spoken. The Romans also brought the new religion of Christianity, which was firmly established throughout the region by A.D. 600.

The sheer size of the Roman Empire made it difficult to govern. In A.D. 330, Emperor Constantine (reigned 306-34) rebuilt the old Greek city of Byzantium and renamed it Constantinople, turning it into his eastern capital. In 395, the empire split in two, and the eastern half was ruled from Constantinople. When the western Roman Empire finally collapsed in 476, the eastern half continued as the Byzantine Empire.

THE BYZANTINE EMPIRE

Although it was strong, the Byzantine Empire faced many external threats. After the 560s, Slavs from eastern Europe moved south toward the Adriatic, cutting off the empire

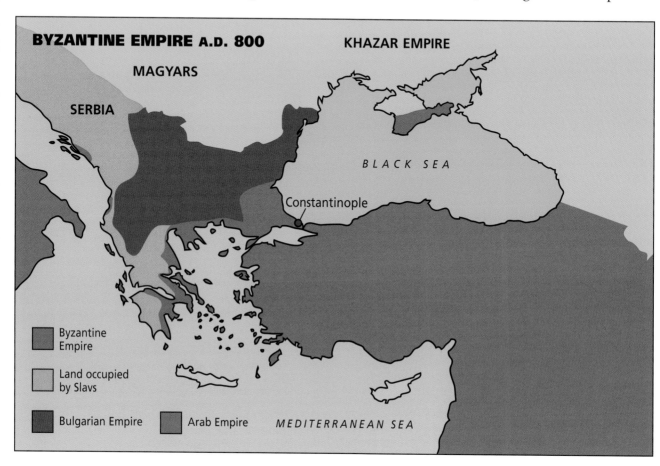

BYZANTINE EMPIRE A.D. 800

KHAZAR EMPIRE

MAGYARS

SERBIA

BLACK SEA

Constantinople

Byzantine Empire

Land occupied by Slavs

Bulgarian Empire

Arab Empire

MEDITERRANEAN SEA

The remains of the basilica in Salona (Solin), Croatia, showing Roman stone columns.

from western Europe. Independent Slav states emerged in Croatia and Serbia. The Bulgars invaded what is now Bulgaria in the late 600s and soon merged with the local Slav population.

The threat from both groups diminished as they gradually converted to Christianity. By 1025, all the Slav and Bulgar states had been conquered and their peoples absorbed into the empire. Although the Byzantine peoples now spoke different languages and wrote in Greek, Cyrillic, and Latin scripts, they were united by the single Orthodox Church. This had finally split from the western Roman Catholic Church in 1054. Only Croatia remained Roman Catholic.

A NEW SCRIPT

In A.D. 863, the Greek missionaries Saints Cyril and Methodius set out to convert the pagan Slavs of central and eastern Europe to Christianity. They translated the Bible and other Christian texts into the Slavic language and developed a new script to write the language down. This Cyrillic script, as it is known, is still used today in the Slav nations of Russia, Serbia, Macedonia, and Bulgaria. But the Croats, who speak the same Serbo-Croat language as the Serbs, used the Latin script in which this book is printed.

This Bulgarian icon depicts Saints Cyril and Methodius with a page of Cyrillic script.

ROMAN AND BYZANTINE RULE

146 B.C. Roman province of Macedonia (modern Greece) established

33 B.C. Romans begin conquest of Dalmatia (Croatia and Bosnia)

C. A.D. 50 St. Paul brings Christianity to Greece

106 Romans conquer modern-day Romania

330 Founding of Constantinople

395 Roman Empire split in two; most of Balkans becomes part of eastern Roman, or Byzantine, Empire

560s Slavs move south into Byzantine Empire

811 Bulgars defeat Byzantine army at Adrianople

863 Saints Cyril and Methodius begin to convert the Slavs to Christianity

865 Boris I of Bulgaria becomes Christian

1025 Byzantine Empire now includes Slavs and Bulgars

1054 Split between Eastern Orthodox and western Catholic churches

OTTOMAN RULE

In 632, Arab armies swept out of the Arabian Peninsula, taking their new religion of Islam with them. By 674, they were at the gates of Constantinople, presenting a military and religious threat to the Byzantine Empire that eventually overwhelmed it.

THE ISLAMIC CONQUEST

The Byzantine armies defeated the Arabs three times, but their empire was successfully invaded in 1070 by the Muslim Seljuk Turks, who conquered most of modern Turkey. Serbia and Bulgaria also broke away to become independent states. By 1250, the Byzantine Empire had lost much of its territory.

In the late 1200s, a new power emerged in Turkey. Then just a small isolated state, it expanded rapidly during the reign of Osman I (c. 1281-1324), after whom the new empire was named. Soon, the whole of Turkey had been conquered. In 1354, the Ottoman Empire gained its first foothold in Europe, and a new era had begun.

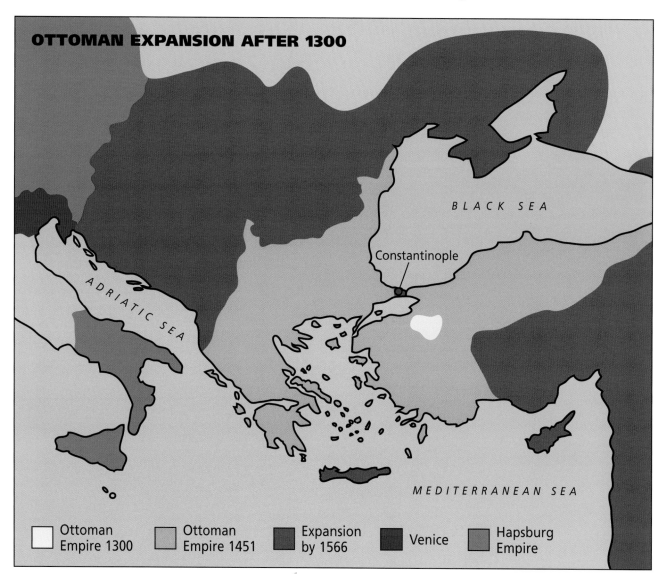

OTTOMAN EXPANSION AFTER 1300

BLACK SEA

Constantinople

ADRIATIC SEA

MEDITERRANEAN SEA

- Ottoman Empire 1300
- Ottoman Empire 1451
- Expansion by 1566
- Venice
- Hapsburg Empire

THE SIEGE OF CONSTANTINOPLE

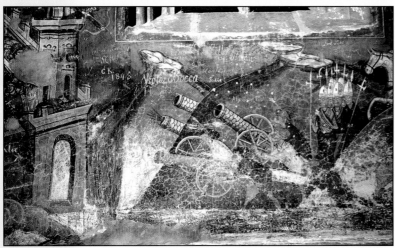

This mural shows the siege of Constantinople in 1453. Graffiti was scratched on it at a later date.

In 1453, the Ottoman Sultan Mehmet II (reigned 1444-81) began the final siege of Constantinople. He blockaded the city and stopped supplies from reaching the city from the Black Sea and Russia. A huge 32-foot (10 m) long cannon—the biggest ever produced at that time—hurled 1,200-pound (550 kg) rocks against the city walls. The siege lasted 46 days, and thousands were killed on both sides. On May 29, the city finally fell, and the Byzantine population gave way to the new Muslim inhabitants.

THE OTTOMAN EMPIRE

After major victories against the Serbs and Bulgarians, the Ottomans eventually captured Constantinople in 1453, bringing the Byzantine Empire to an end. This new Ottoman Empire was vast. Soon stretching from the Persian Gulf in the east to Hungary in the west, and along the entire length of North Africa, it contained many different peoples and religions.

The Ottoman sultan ruled this empire through the skillful use of local people to govern the different provinces. Talented persons were promoted to positions of high power, for there was no hereditary Ottoman nobility to run the empire.

Such officials kept their own languages and customs, but they all converted to Islam (as did about one-fifth of the population of the Balkans) so that they would prosper in the new regime.

The Ottomans were tolerant of other religions. They respected Christians and Jews as "people of the Book," for all three religions honor the God of the Bible and Koran. Christians paid higher taxes than Muslims, but across the Balkans, relations between Muslims, Orthodox Christians, and Catholics remained peaceful. So, under Ottoman rule, the Balkan region was well run, and for the first time in more than 500 years, it was united.

THE RISE OF OTTOMAN POWER

632 Arab armies spread Islam across Middle East

674-78, 717-18, 863 Arab armies threaten Byzantine Empire

1071 Byzantines defeated by the Seljuk Turks at the Battle of Manzikert in eastern Turkey

1200s Serbia and Bulgaria become independent states

c. 1281-1324 Ottoman Empire created under Osman I

1354 Ottoman Turks capture Gallipoli, their first toehold in Europe

1361 Ottomans move capital to the European city of Adrianople in Thrace

1389 Serb army defeated at Battle of Kosovo Polje

1393 Ottomans conquer Bulgaria

1453 Ottomans capture Constantinople and make it their capital

1566 Sultan Suleiman the Magnificent dies; Ottoman power at its height

THE START OF THE "EASTERN QUESTION"

In 1683, the Ottoman Turks stood at the gates of Vienna. They were at the height of their power and dominated the entire Balkans. Over the next 200 years, however, control of the region gradually slipped away from them.

The siege of Vienna, 1683.

AUSTRIA AND RUSSIA

As the Ottomans continued their expansion into central Europe during the 17th century, they came into conflict with the Roman Catholic Hapsburg rulers of Austria. In 1683, the Ottomans besieged the Austrian capital, Vienna, but were themselves attacked and heavily defeated. Austria then went on the offensive and, by 1699, made huge gains in Hungary, Croatia, and Transylvania (northern Romania). Further victories brought them control of Serbia in 1718.

The Ottomans also faced a threat from Russia, the leading Orthodox state. Russia captured Ottoman territories around the Black Sea, thereby winning the right to intervene in the Ottoman Empire to ensure good government for Romania and to protect the rights of Orthodox Christians living under Ottoman rule. Catherine the Great of Russia (reigned 1762-96) and Emperor Joseph II of Austria (reigned 1780-90) even drew up a plan to divide the Balkans between them, although nothing came of it.

THE "EASTERN QUESTION"

As Ottoman power declined during the 18th and 19th centuries, discontent inside the empire rose. In 1804, Muslim army officers murdered the Vizier of Belgrade, the sultan's representative in Serbia, because of

THE GREEK WAR OF INDEPENDENCE

In 1821, Greek nationalists rose against their Ottoman rulers and appealed to European nations for help. Many people saw the Greeks as Christian freedom fighters battling Ottoman tyranny and pressed their governments to assist. At first, the Greeks did well, but in 1826, the Turkish army defeated them. In 1827, Britain, France, and Russia destroyed the Ottoman navy at Navarino, while the Russians advanced on Constantinople. The Ottomans were forced into peace talks, and Greek independence followed in 1830.

The battle of Navarino, 1827.

his pro-Christian views. They also massacred his Christian Serb supporters, who in turn appealed to the sultan for help. But the sultan refused to arm Christian subjects against his fellow Muslims, so the Christian Serbs asked Russia for help. Russia, however, was occupied with its lengthy war against Napoleon and could not support the Serbs. The revolt was crushed. A second revolt succeeded, and in 1817, Serbia became autonomous.

To the south of Serbia, the Greeks also rose in revolt and eventually won their independence. In 1829, Russia occupied southern and eastern Romania. Ottoman Turkey had lost so much power that it was regarded as "the sick man of Europe" by the other European states. The "Eastern Question"—how to handle the inevitable Ottoman collapse—dominated European politics for the next century.

> *"The more one thinks about the immense question of the fall of the Turkish Empire, the more one plunges into a labyrinth of difficulty and complications."*
>
> **Count Nesselrode, Russian foreign minister, 1829**

OTTOMAN DECLINE

1683 Turks defeated at Vienna

1699 By the Treaty of Karlowitz, Turks lose Hungary, Croatia, and Transylvania to Austria, and most of the Adriatic coastline of Croatia to Venice

1718 Turks lose Serbia to Austria, although the southern half, including Belgrade, is won back in 1739

1770 Greek revolt crushed by Ottomans

1774 Russia wins right to intervene in Ottoman affairs

1804-14 First, unsuccessful Serb revolt

1815 Austria gains lengthy Adriatic coastline from Venice at end of Napoleonic Wars

1815-17 A second Serb revolt leads to Serbian autonomy within the weakened Ottoman Empire

1821-30 Greek War of Independence

1828-29 Russo-Turkish war leads to full self-government for Serbia and Russian military occupation of Moldavia and Wallachia in Romania

REDRAWING THE MAP

In 1878, the major European powers redrew the map of the Balkans, massively reducing Ottoman control over the region. The controversy this caused embittered relations between the Balkan states for years to come.

THE BULGARIAN REVOLT

By the 1870s, the largest part of the Balkans still under Ottoman control were the countries now called Bulgaria and Macedonia. Revolutionary groups were active in stirring up opposition to Ottoman rule in the region, but peasant uprisings, such as the one in April 1876, usually had little chance of success. On this occasion, however, the sultan was alarmed by the revolt, and his army swiftly and brutally repressed it.

News of their atrocities spread around Europe. All of the major European nations called for the sultan to introduce reforms that would prevent future revolts. Russia, in particular, was outraged by what had happened, because it supported the Bulgarians as fellow Orthodox Slavs. When the sultan refused to make reforms, Russia invaded the Balkans in 1877 and advanced on Constantinople.

SAN STEFANO

In early 1878, the sultan was forced to make peace with the Russians. By the Treaty of San Stefano, the sultan agreed to the independence of Serbia, Montenegro (a tiny principality on the Adriatic coast), and Romania. He also agreed to a vast new autonomous Bulgarian state, stretching across both Bulgaria and Macedonia, with an outlet to the Aegean Sea. Russian troops were to be stationed in Bulgaria for two years.

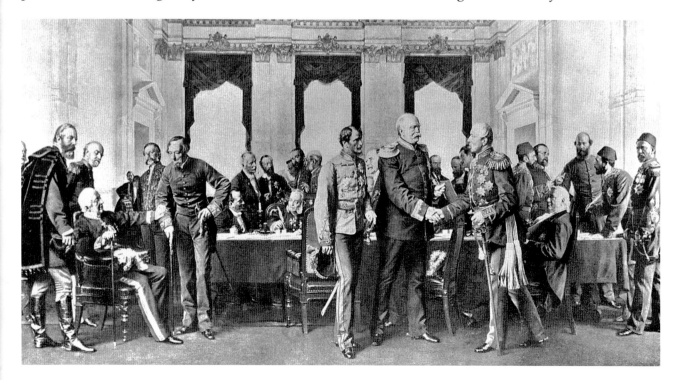

European leaders met at the Congress of Berlin in 1878 to decide the fate of the Balkans.

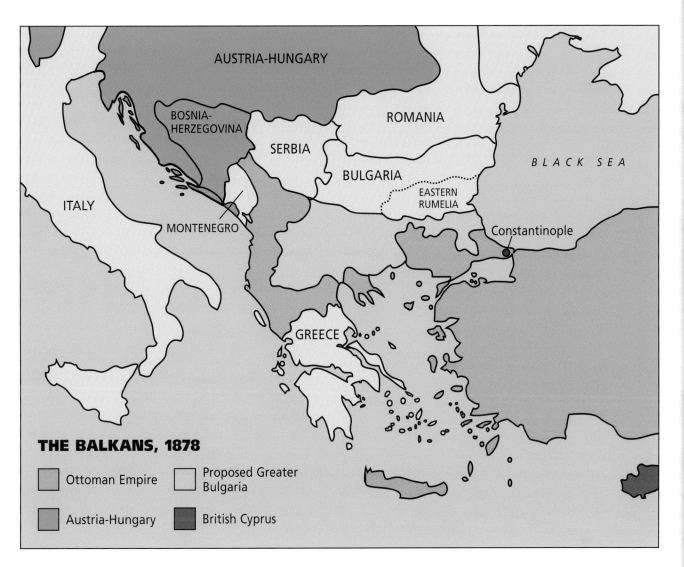

THE BALKANS, 1878

- ☐ Ottoman Empire
- ☐ Proposed Greater Bulgaria
- ☐ Austria-Hungary
- ☐ British Cyprus

CONGRESS OF BERLIN

The huge influence this treaty gave Russia was unacceptable to the rest of Europe, and a revised treaty was forced through. This cut Bulgaria to half its proposed size, with a new buffer state—Eastern Rumelia—inserted between it and Constantinople. Macedonia returned to Ottoman rule, Austria occupied Bosnia-Herzegovina, and Britain occupied the Mediterranean island of Cyprus.

But the Bulgarians never forgot that they had been promised a vast new state and dreamed of regaining the "lost lands" of Macedonia.

THE WEAKENING OF OTTOMAN POWER

1841 Peasant uprising in Bulgaria

1848 Russians and Ottomans put down uprisings in Moldavia and Wallachia

1854-56 Britain and France support Ottoman Empire against Russia;

Russian troops forced out of Moldavia and Wallachia

1859 Moldavia and Wallachia unite as semi-independent Romania

1876 Ottomans brutally crush Bulgarian uprising

1877-78 Russia fights Ottoman Empire to support Bulgarians

March 1878 Treaty of San Stefano creates a greater Bulgaria

July 1878 European powers force new borders on Bulgaria at Congress of Berlin

1881 Greece gains further lands

1885 Eastern Rumelia becomes part of Bulgaria

1908 Bulgaria becomes fully independent

THE END OF OTTOMAN RULE

The events of 1878 redrew the map of the Balkans but left many Balkan people, notably those in Macedonia, under foreign rule. Two more wars were fought before this issue was finally resolved.

THE MACEDONIAN PROBLEM

Macedonia was the ancient home of Alexander the Great, but the region had no clear borders and no official existence within the Ottoman Empire. It was surrounded by Greece to its south and Serbia and Bulgaria to its north and included parts of what are now Greece, Albania, Serbia and Montenegro, Macedonia, and Bulgaria. As the last major part of Europe under Ottoman rule, Macedonia was coveted by Austria-Hungary (that empire's official name since 1867), Russia, and Italy, as well as by Greece and Serbia. Bulgaria still dreamed of annexing it, thereby establishing the Greater Bulgaria it had been promised at San Stefano. Most of the region's people were Macedonians, but there were also large Greek, Bulgarian, Serb, Albanian, and other populations. Most were Orthodox, but there were also many Roman Catholics and Muslims, and the largest single group in the capital of Salonika was Jewish.

Political groups in Macedonia were split between those who wanted autonomy, or full independence from Ottoman rule, and those who wanted to join neighboring states. Bulgarian Macedonians seeking autonomy formed the first major nationalist organization in the area—the Internal Macedonian Revolutionary Organization (IMRO)—but most Bulgarians wanted to join Bulgaria itself. By 1911, there were more than 200 competing armed groups active in the region.

THE YOUNG TURKS

In July 1908, a group of liberal Ottoman army officers—the "Young Turks"—tried to force modernization on the Ottoman Empire. In response, the sultan restored the liberal constitution he had suspended during the Russo-Turkish War, which allowed all Ottoman men to vote, regardless of their religion or ethnicity. Bosnia-Herzegovina was then under Austrian control, although still part of the Ottoman Empire, and Austria feared Bosnian rights would follow. So Austria took over complete control of Bosnia, to the dismay of Serbia and Russia— neither wanted further Austrian expansion in the area.

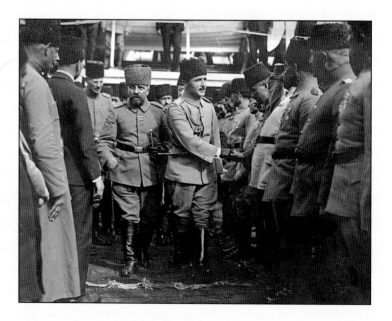

Enver Pasha (1879-1922), center, leader of the "Young Turks," greets Ottoman troops during a tour of inspection.

Bulgarian troops enter a Serbian town in 1912 during the First Balkan War.

THE FIRST TWO BALKAN WARS

In 1911, Albanian Macedonians began a successful rebellion. Serbia and Montenegro, Bulgaria, and Greece quickly invaded to keep other countries from seizing Macedonia and divided it among themselves. Serbia and Greece got the most, and Bulgaria was unhappy with the result. In a second war in 1913, Bulgaria fought its former allies and its Ottoman enemy, losing many of its previous gains as a result. By the end of 1913, Ottoman rule was almost at an end. The Balkans were now divided between a triumphant Greece and Serbia and a resentful Bulgaria.

THE FIRST BALKAN WAR

BULGARIA

OTTOMAN EMPIRE

AEGEAN SEA

GREECE

to Bulgaria
to Serbia
Albania
to Greece
to Montenegro
to Ottoman Empire
to Romania

BULGARIA'S LOSSES AFTER SECOND WAR

ROMANIA

BULGARIA

OTTOMAN RULE ENDS

1893 IMRO formed

1898 Aegean island of Crete gains independence from Ottoman rule

1903 IMRO leads major revolt in Macedonia, prompting fierce Ottoman reprisals

1908 Young Turks force reforms,

prompting Austria to annex Bosnia-Herzegovina

1911 Albanian revolt begins; rebels demand independence

1911-12 Italian-Ottoman war: Italians seize Dodecanese Islands

October 1912 First

Balkan War: Serbia, Greece, Bulgaria, and Montenegro invade Macedonia

May 1913 Treaty of London ends First Balkan War: Ottoman Empire reduced to a strip of land around Constantinople, Albania becomes independent

June-July 1913 Second

Balkan War as Bulgaria fights Greece, Serbia, Romania, and Ottoman Empire for more of Macedonia

August 1913 Treaty of Bucharest; Bulgaria loses land to Romania, Ottomans, Greece, and Serbia

1913 Crete joins Greece

WORLD WAR I

The first two Balkan Wars of 1912-13 ended Ottoman rule over the Balkans but left the region in a volatile state. The "Third Balkan War," which started in 1914, engulfed the entire world.

THE NEW BOSNIAN CRISIS

Austria-Hungary was just as much a loser in the first two Balkan Wars as the Ottoman Empire. Although it had annexed Bosnia-Herzegovina in 1908, Austria-Hungary had failed to pacify its largely pro-Serb population, who wanted to unite with Serbia. They quickly formed secret societies to fight against Austrian rule. For its part, Serbia wanted to unite all the so-called South Slavs living under Austrian rule and was hugely encouraged by its successes in the first two Balkan Wars.

THE THIRD BALKAN WAR

On June 28, 1914, the heir to the Austrian throne, Archduke Franz Ferdinand, was assassinated in the Bosnian capital of Sarajevo. Austria blamed Serbia for the assassination and issued harsh demands to Serbia. Serbia agreed to most of the terms because it was exhausted after its recent wars, but Austria wanted to crush Serbia and so declared war.

The third Balkan War became much bigger. European alliances meant that Germany supported Austria, and Russia, France, Britain, and Montenegro supported Serbia. By August 1914, World War I had begun.

> **"We have got either to annihilate Serbia or, if we cannot do that, learn to love it."**
>
> **J. Baernreither, Austrian political commentator, 1914**

Assassin Gavrilo Princip under arrest shortly after murdering Archduke Franz Ferdinand in Sarajevo.

TAKING SIDES

For the Balkan nations, this third war was a continuation of the first two. The Ottoman Empire joined the Central Powers of Austria and Germany because of its fear of Russia. Bulgaria joined them because they promised to return the land lost in 1912-13. Romania joined the opposing Allies because it hoped to gain land, while Greece joined them because it feared losing recent gains to Bulgaria and the Ottomans. Albania remained neutral.

In fact, the outcome of the war was decided on a wider European scale. Serbia, Greece, and Romania ended up on the winning side, while the Ottoman Empire, Austria-Hungary, and Bulgaria were the losers.

THE BALKANS AND WORLD WAR I

GERMANY

RUSSIA

AUSTRIA-HUNGARY

SWITZERLAND

Bosnia-Herzegovina

ROMANIA

Sarajevo

SERBIA

BLACK SEA

ITALY

BULGARIA

MONTENEGRO

ALBANIA

GREECE

OTTOMAN EMPIRE

☐ Neutral countries

☐ Allies in 1914

☐ Countries joining Allies during the war

☐ Central Powers in 1914

☐ Countries joining Central Powers during the war

CYPRUS

THE COURSE OF THE WAR

June 1914 Assassination of Archduke Franz Ferdinand in Sarajevo

July 1914 Austria declares war on Serbia

August 1914 World War I begins

October 1914 Ottoman Empire joins Central Powers

April 1915-January 1916 Allied troops occupy Gallipoli, close to Constantinople

October 1915 Allied troops occupy Salonika in neutral Greece

October 1915 Bulgaria joins Central Powers

December 1915 Serbia overrun by Austrian,

German, and Bulgarian forces

January 1916 Montenegro overrun by Austrian forces

August 1916 Romania joins Allies

December 1916 Romania occupied by Austrian and German troops

June 1917 Greece joins Allies

September 1918 Allies attack Bulgaria; Bulgarian army collapses and Bulgaria makes peace with Allies

October 1918 Ottoman and Austrian empires make peace with Allies

November 1918 Germany agrees to armistice

THE BALKANS BETWEEN THE WARS

The end of World War I once again redrew the map of the Balkans. Old empires disappeared, and new nations appeared in their place.

NEW BORDERS

After the defeat and collapse of the Austro-Hungarian, Russian, and Ottoman empires, the Balkan map was redrawn yet again. Romania gained Bessarabia (now Moldova) from Russia and Transylvania from Austria-Hungary, thereby doubling its former size. Bulgaria lost its access to the Aegean Sea to Greece. The new state of Yugoslavia emerged from the remnants of Austria-Hungary.

REFUGEES

These changes caused vast numbers of refugees to flee from their old homes and seek safety with their fellow nationals. More than 280,000 Hungarians fled from Romania and Yugoslavia, while 270,000 Bulgarians fled from Bulgaria's neighbors. The biggest migration involved Greeks and Turks. About 1.35 million Greeks fled from

THE POSTWAR BALKANS

THE CREATION OF YUGOSLAVIA

In 1917, Croats and Serbs living under Austrian rule formed a Yugoslav National Committee to unite all "South Slavs" living in the Austrian Empire. With the defeat of Austria-Hungary in October 1918, the Kingdom of the Serbs, Croats, and Slovenes was proclaimed. Serbia and Montenegro merged with the former Austrian provinces of Bosnia, Croatia, Dalmatia, and Slovenia. The new kingdom was based in Belgrade, with King Peter I of Serbia as ruler. In 1929, a royal Serbian dictatorship was established under Peter's successor, Alexander II, and the country was renamed Yugoslavia.

A photograph of Alexander II taken in 1916.

Troops assemble in a street in Bucharest, Romania, to crush a demonstration in the 1920s.

the new Turkish Republic, and 585,000 Turks fled from Greece and elsewhere in the Balkans. Despite these vast population shifts, 28 percent of the Romanian population and 20 percent of the Bulgarian population were minority groups, while almost one-quarter of all those living in Greece were refugees.

Such vast numbers of people—many with a hatred of their former rulers and an unfamiliarity with their new countries— caused enormous problems in all five Balkan states. Minorities were persecuted, and many people were forced to change their names.

NEW PROBLEMS

Economically and politically, the Balkans faced huge difficulties. The years of war and the cost of postwar reconstruction kept all the national economies weak.

Parliamentary government failed to resolve these issues, and this led to military coups in Greece, conflict between Serbs and Croats in Yugoslavia, political assassinations in Bulgaria, and dictatorial rule in Albania.

In 1929, the New York Stock Exchange crashed, causing a worldwide economic slump. The Balkan economies all collapsed, bringing right-wing (often royal) dictatorships in Yugoslavia, Bulgaria, Greece, and Romania. All dissent was crushed.

THE INTER-WAR YEARS

1918 Kingdom of the Serbs, Croats, and Slovenes established

1919 Treaty of Neuilly establishes new smaller borders of Bulgaria

1920 Treaty of Trianon gives Transylvania and other regions to Romania; large areas given to Kingdom of the Serbs

1920 Treaty of Sèvres gives parts of western Turkey to Greece; new government of Kemal Ataturk rejects treaty

1922 Ottoman Empire ends

1923 Lausanne Treaty rewrites Sèvres in Turkey's favor; population exchanges agreed on between

Greece and Turkey; Turkey becomes a republic

1924 Ahmed Bey Zog takes over Albania, becomes King Zog I in 1928

1929 Kingdom of the Serbs renamed Yugoslavia; King Alexander II establishes royal dictatorship

1930 King Carol of Romania finances fascist Iron Guard movement

1936 King Boris establishes royal dictatorship in Bulgaria

1936 King George II of Greece accepts right-wing dictatorship of General Metaxas

WORLD WAR II

In 1922, Mussolini and his Fascist Party took power in Italy; in 1933, Hitler's Nazi Party gained control in Germany. Both leaders threatened the Balkans.

INVASIONS

Italy already controlled land around the edge of the Mediterranean but dreamed of a new Roman Empire that would turn that sea into an "Italian lake." In 1939, Italy invaded Albania. After joining the war on the German side, Italy also invaded Greece in 1940. The Italian army was, however, swiftly defeated and pushed back into Albania.

Germany's aim in the region was to safeguard its vital oil supplies from Romania and to protect its armies when they eventually invaded the USSR. By early 1941, Germany had allied itself with pro-fascist Romania and Bulgaria and pressured Yugoslavia to do the same. The Yugoslavs reluctantly agreed, but two days later, a coup overthrew the government and its leaders rejected the agreement. Nine days later, Nazi Germany invaded Yugoslavia and Greece.

THE BALKANS IN WORLD WAR II

A German soldier searches a Bosnian Muslim in Sarajevo after the 1941 Nazi invasion.

The Nazi occupation had a huge effect throughout the Balkans. Croatia became an independent state run by an extreme nationalist party, the Ustase, which persecuted the Serbs, killing several hundred thousand of them in concentration camps. Serb Chetnik resistance fighters retaliated by killing thousands of Croats in Bosnia, while Bulgarian troops invaded northern Greece and killed many thousands of Greeks.

Borders were rearranged to settle old scores: Bulgaria gained land it had lost in 1913 and 1919; Romania lost land to Bulgaria, Hungary, and the USSR; and Yugoslavia was entirely dismantled. Everywhere, Jews, Gypsies, communists, and other minorities were persecuted and often sent to their deaths.

THE YUGOSLAV RESISTANCE

Of all the resistance movements against German domination of Europe, the Yugoslav one was the most effective. At first, the main group was the Chetniks, named after Serbian guerrillas who had fought against Ottoman rule. The Chetniks were Serbian nationalists and vehemently pro-royalist and anti-communist.

The other group consisted of the Yugoslav communist partisans of Josip Broz Tito (1892-1980), based mainly in the mountains of Bosnia and Montenegro. Both groups were predominantly Serb. Britain at first supported the Chetniks but changed allegiance in early 1944. Tito's forces employed local knowledge in their fight against German forces and liberated Belgrade and the rest of the country with minimal Red Army support.

Josip Tito as a resistance fighter in 1942.

LIBERATION

The German invasion of the USSR in 1941 was a turning point in the war. Although initially successful, the German army was defeated at Stalingrad in 1943, and the Soviet Red Army went on the offensive. By September 1944, the Red Army had liberated Romania and Bulgaria, both of which then changed sides and fought the rest of the war against Germany.

British troops liberated Greece, while communist-led resistance movements in both Albania and Yugoslavia expelled the Italians and Germans. By early 1945, all areas except northeast Yugoslavia were liberated.

> *"Henceforth 100 prisoners or hostages to be shot for every soldier killed and 50 for every one wounded. Every regional garrison to arrest as many communists, nationalists, democrats, and Jews as possible. . . ."*
>
> **German High Command instructions to its army in Serbia, October 1941**

WORLD WAR II IN THE BALKANS

April 1939 Italy invades Albania

September 1939 Start of World War II; Germany invades Poland; Britain and France declare war on Germany

May 1940 Italy joins war on German side

September 1940 Germany, Italy, and Japan sign Tripartite Pact

October 1940 Italy invades Greece

November 1940 Romania joins Tripartite Pact

March 1941 Bulgaria joins Tripartite Pact

April 1941 Germany invades Yugoslavia and Greece

June 1941 Romanian forces join German invasion of USSR

January 1943 German advance into USSR halted at Stalingrad

September 1944 Romania and Bulgaria are liberated by Red Army and change

sides in war

October 1944 Athens liberated by British army

October 1944 Tito's partisans join with Red Army to liberate Belgrade

May 1945 Germany's defeat ends war in Europe

THE COMING OF COMMUNISM

In both Romania and Bulgaria, communist parties loyal to Moscow were in power by 1947. They transformed both countries, at the expense of individual freedom and national liberty.

COMMUNIST CONTROL

When the Red Army entered the Balkans in 1944, both Romania and Bulgaria changed sides and declared war on Germany, their former ally. Romanian forces fought beside the Russians in Hungary, sustaining 150,000 casualties, while Bulgarian forces fought in Macedonia, with 32,000 casualties.

Russia at first supported King Michael of Romania (reigned 1927-30, 1940-47) but soon enforced the agreement they had with Churchill (see box) to dominate the country. They built up the local Communist Party, which only had about 1,000 members in 1944, into an organization of more than 200,000 by 1947 and forced the king to include communists in his government. In 1946, the communists swept to power in a rigged general election. King Michael abdicated the following year, and the country became a People's Republic, completing the communist takeover.

In Bulgaria, the Soviet takeover was as quick. The Communist Party grew rapidly from 14,000 in 1944 to 422,000 in 1946. Its leader, Georgi Dimitrov (1882-1949),

> *"From Stettin in the Baltic to Trieste in the Adriatic, an Iron Curtain has descended across the continent."*
>
> **Winston Churchill, former British prime minister, 1946**

DIVIDING THE BALKANS

In October 1944, British Prime Minister Winston Churchill (1874-1965) met Soviet leader Joseph Stalin (1879-1953) in Moscow to discuss the war. Churchill was concerned about possible conflicts between the two allies in the Balkans and proposed to divide the area between them. The USSR would dominate in Romania with 90 percent control, while Britain and the United States would get 10 percent. These figures were reversed for Greece, where Britain and the U.S. got 90 percent and the USSR 10 percent.

Churchill proposed a 50-50 split in Hungary and Yugoslavia and a 75-25 split in the Soviets' favor in Bulgaria. Stalin agreed. Thus the postwar future of the Balkans was decided without consulting any Balkan nation.

attacked opposition parties and tortured, tried, and executed thousands of opponents in People's Courts. In September 1946, he established a republic and took full control the following year.

DIVIDING LINES

In power, the communists nationalized every industry, expanded industrial production, merged farms into state-run collectives, and mechanized agriculture. New road and rail systems were built, mass housing estates were constructed, and electricity was brought to every town. The

Blocks of apartments go up in Bucharest in 1957 as the Romanian capital expands under communist rule.

results were impressive. Industrial and agricultural productivity soared and towns boomed—Bucharest and Sofia, the two capitals, both doubled in size by 1990. But all this was only achieved through rigid communist control over every aspect of daily life. Opposition parties were banned, dissent was crushed, and freedom of speech and religion were denied.

Politically, Bulgaria remained Moscow's most loyal ally in the Balkans. Romania, in contrast, took a more independent line, especially after Nicolae Ceausescu (1918-89) became party leader and promoted the independence of his country. Both countries, however, remained firmly behind the Iron Curtain that divided Soviet-dominated eastern Europe from the rest of the continent.

SOVIET DOMINATION

September 1944
Red Army liberates Romania and Bulgaria; both change sides and fight Germany

October 1944
Moscow Agreement between Churchill and Stalin to divide the Balkans between the USSR and Britain/U.S.

September 1946
Communists establish republic in Bulgaria

November 1946
Communists win Romanian general election

February 1947 Paris peace treaties settle Balkan borders: Yugoslavia gains Adriatic territories and Greece gains Dodecanese

Islands from Italy; Bulgaria and Romania regain old borders, although Romania loses land to USSR and Bulgaria

September 1947 Communists take full control in Bulgaria

December 1947 King Michael of Romania abdicates; country becomes a People's Republic

1949 Romania and Bulgaria join Comecon—which ties their economies to the USSR

1955 Romania and Bulgaria join Warsaw Pact

1965 Romania's new leader Ceausescu follows independent line in foreign policy

YUGOSLAVIA AND ALBANIA

Josip Tito in Yugoslavia and Enver Hoxha in Albania were both charismatic leaders. Their unique versions of communist rule lasted for more than 35 years, until their deaths.

COMMUNIST YUGOSLAVIA

After the liberation of Yugoslavia, Tito moved quickly to establish communist control. His partisans pursued up to 200,000 Ustase troops and civilians attempting to flee to safety in Austria and killed at least 110,000 of them. Serb Chetniks and Slovenian collaborators were murdered, along with other enemies, in a campaign that, by 1947, saw at least 200,000 deaths, many in former Nazi camps. Elections held in November 1945 were rigged to communist advantage, giving them control

in Yugoslavia before the rest of the Balkans. A federal republic was established, consisting of the six republics: Bosnia-Herzegovina, Croatia, Macedonia, Montenegro, Serbia, and Slovenia.

Tito was an ardent communist, but he was not prepared to accept orders from Stalin. He knew that the Soviet leader would put Soviet political interests in the Balkans above both the interests of Yugoslavia and Tito's own party. In June 1948, the USSR and its allies froze all economic and other cooperation with Yugoslavia, expecting Tito to change his policies. He refused, and Yugoslavia now stood alone.

> "By saying 'No!' to Stalin, Tito stood on his own two feet. . . . From that moment on, Tito represented the sun for most Yugoslavs."
>
> Kosta Cavoski, Yugoslav historian, 1990

"POSITIVE NEUTRALITY"

Tito faced many problems in Yugoslavia. The country was threatened with invasion by the USSR and its allies. It had a major border dispute with Italy over the Adriatic port of Trieste and disputes about borders and ethnic minorities with most of its other neighbors. It also faced internal conflict between Croats and Serbs, and Albanians and Serbs. Tito addressed these issues by putting Yugoslav nationalism above local

Josip Tito in 1953.

loyalties, sharing power among the six republics, and balancing competing interests.

Tito's unique form of socialism allowed workers to "self-manage" industries and loosened party control over daily life. He made Yugoslavia the leader of the world's non-aligned nations and championed "positive neutrality" and "active coexistence" with both sides during the Cold War.

Free to buy and sell: Yugoslav women purchase fruit at an outdoor market during the Tito years.

ALBANIA

Enver Hoxha addresses a rally in 1945.

Resistance to Italian rule in Albania was led by Enver Hoxha (1908-85) and his communist-dominated National Liberation Army. After liberation in 1944, Hoxha established a communist republic and remained slavishly loyal to Stalin and the USSR—even breaking with his powerful neighbor, Tito, when Stalin did in 1948. When the new Soviet leader, Nikita Khrushchev, denounced Stalin in 1956, Hoxha shifted his loyalties to China. From then on, Albania pursued a rigorous pro-China policy. Thousands were killed in political purges, religion was banned, and foreign travel was forbidden.

YUGOSLAVIA AND ALBANIA

1944 Albania liberated; Enver Hoxha establishes a communist-led republic

1945 Yugoslav communists win rigged elections and take full control

1946 Yugoslav constitution creates

six federal republics, with two autonomous provinces of Kosovo and Vojvodina in Serbia

1948 Tito-Stalin split; Albania, Romania, and Bulgaria all break with Yugoslavia

1949 Comecon founded—with

Albania as member—to enforce economic boycott of Yugoslavia

1953 Stalin dies

1955 Yugoslavia and the USSR resume "fraternal relations"

1955 Warsaw Pact founded with Albania as member

1956 Albania breaks with USSR and aligns with China

1961 Albania excluded from Comecon; withdraws from Warsaw Pact in 1968

1980 Tito dies

1985 Hoxha dies

29

POSTWAR GREECE

Alone among the Balkan countries, Greece did not become communist, but it suffered years of political instability before it became a fully-functioning democracy.

CIVIL WAR

After the Nazi occupation of Greece in 1941, rival royalist and communist groups fought the Germans. After liberation, they fought each other. Churchill and Stalin had agreed that Greece was to be under British, rather than Soviet, influence. When civil war broke out in 1946 between the two groups, Stalin refused to help the communists and objected to Yugoslavia's support for them—one of the main reasons for his split with Tito in 1948.

The three-year civil war was brutal and left a deeper psychological wound than World War II. Under a series of right-wing governments led by Constantine Karamanlis (1907-98), Greece had massive economic

> *"The revolution in Greece must be crushed and the sooner, the better."*
>
> **Stalin on the Greek communist forces in the civil war, February 1948**

support from the U.S.—more than $3 billion by 1963—and began to develop tourism. But the dispute with Turkey about the future of Cyprus poisoned postwar politics. Greeks living on the island, then a British colony, wanted *enosis* (union with Greece), which was opposed by Turkey. Cyprus became independent in 1960, but Greek and Turkish relations remained tense.

THE GREEK CIVIL WAR

The communist-led resistance movement, EAM (the National Liberation Front), wanted a communist revolution in Greece and opposed the return of the monarchy. After bitter clashes with royalist resistance forces in the winter of 1944-45, the two sides agreed to a truce that left two-thirds of Greece in EAM hands.

In 1946, the truce broke down, and civil war began. The communists were supported by Yugoslavia, Albania, and Bulgaria, all acting against Stalin's express wishes, while the Greek royalist army received help from Britain and the U.S. The war lasted three years. About 30,000 people lost their lives in the fighting.

A convoy of Greek peasants during the war.

THE COLONELS' REGIME

During the 1960s, the left-wing Center Union Party of George Papandreou (1888-1968) gained strength. But when it looked likely to win a decisive election victory in 1967, the Greek army, led by Colonel George Papadopoulos (1919-99) and others, staged a military coup. King Constantine II (ruled 1964-73) went into exile, and a republic was declared in 1973.

The colonels suppressed civil liberties and imprisoned their opponents. There was widespread international criticism of the new regime.

George Papandreou.

MODERN GREECE

The colonels' regime collapsed in 1974 when it offered support to a pro-*enosis* coup in Cyprus against the elected government. Constantine Karamanlis returned from exile, and a new republican constitution was put in place.

From then on, Greece became a model two-party democracy. Conservative governments alternated with the left-wing Panhellenic Socialist Movement (PASOK), which first won power in 1981. A member of the European Union (EU) since 1981, Greece has now become a fully integrated—and an increasingly rich—western European country.

Constantine Karamanlis.

MODERN GREECE

April 1941 Nazis occupy Greece

1942 Rival monarchist and communist groups start guerrilla war against German forces

October 1944 Moscow Agreement between Churchill and Stalin on the postwar future of Greece; British forces liberate Athens

1944-45 Fierce clashes between communist and royalist forces

February 1945 Truce of Varkiza leaves two-thirds of country under communist control

May 1946-October 1949 Greek Civil War

September 1946 Greek referendum to restore

monarchy; George II returns to the throne

1952 Greece joins the defensive North Atlantic Treaty Organization (NATO) along with other western European nations and the U.S.

1955 Constantine Karamanlis first becomes Greek prime minister

1967-74 Army regime rules Greece

1973 Greece becomes a republic

1975 New constitution establishes the democratic Hellenic Republic

1981 Joins EU; PASOK Socialist Party wins its first general election

THE END OF COMMUNISM

In 1985, a new leader took power in the Soviet Union. Within five years, communist rule in the Balkans had come to a dramatic, and sometimes violent, end.

GLASNOST

When Mikhail Gorbachev (1931-) took power, the USSR had fallen well behind the U.S. and other western countries in its wealth and standard of living. Gorbachev wanted to break with the hard-line policies of his predecessors and reform the communist system to make it work better. He proposed to do this through the twin polices of *glasnost* (openness) and *perestroika* (reconstruction).

At first, these new policies had little impact on the Balkans. But in December 1988, Gorbachev addressed the United Nations (UN) in New York. He announced a massive reduction of 500,000 men in the Red Army and made it clear that communist parties in eastern Europe could no longer rely on

"Profound transformations must be carried out in the economy and the entire system of social relations, and a qualitatively higher standard of living must be ensured."

Mikhail Gorbachev, setting out his agenda before he became Soviet leader, December 1984

Soviet forces to crush dissent, as they had in Czechoslovakia in 1968. Communist governments now had "freedom of choice" and could act without the USSR. Soviet troops began to go home.

DEMOCRATIC ALBANIA

After Enver Hoxha's death in 1985, Albania began to emerge from its isolation. An opposition party was formed, and multi-party elections were held in March 1991. The communists, now renamed the Socialist Party, easily won and introduced more reforms but lost heavily in 1992 to the Democratic Party, whose leader, Sali Berisha (1943-) became the first non-communist president since 1944. In 1997, a government-backed investment plan collapsed, and riots broke out. People armed themselves with stolen weapons. Many thousands fled to Italy before an international force helped restore order.

Albanian refugees crowd onto a boat in 1997.

Romanian demonstrators on top of a tank during the collapse of communist rule in December 1989.

THE END OF COMMUNISM

The effect was immediate. Hungary promised multi-party elections, a non-communist government took power in Poland, and, most dramatically, the Berlin Wall—symbol of divided Europe—was torn down. Romania and Bulgaria resisted this tide of reform, but in December 1989, a violent uprising broke out in Romania. Its leader, Nicolae Ceausescu, was unable to restore order and was arrested and executed after a quick trial. Four days later, Romania dropped its socialist status and removed all communist

signs. An interim government, the National Salvation Front, organized elections, which it won by a landslide in May 1990. A new democratic constitution was established, guaranteeing human rights to all citizens, as well as a free market economy.

In Bulgaria, the communist leader Todor Zhivkov (1911-98) had already begun some reforms, claiming that his policy of *preustroistvo* was reconstructing the state in the same way as the USSR's *perestroika*. Few supported him, however, and he resigned. The one-party system was abolished, and elections were held in June 1990. One-party rule in the Balkans was at an end.

Property of Dexter Middle School Library

THE END OF COMMUNISM

March 1985 Gorbachev takes power in the USSR

April 1985 Enver Hoxha dies in Albania

July 1987 Zhivkov begins reforms in Bulgaria

December 1988 USSR signals end of Soviet power in eastern Europe

September 1989 Poland elects non-communist government

November 1989 Zhivkov forced to resign in Bulgaria

November 1989 Berlin Wall comes down

December 1989 One-party system

abolished in Bulgaria

December 1989 Romania's Ceausescu and his wife Elena executed on Christmas Day

January 1990 First reforms introduced in Albania

May 1990 Democratic elections in Romania

June 1990 Democratic elections in Bulgaria

March 1991 Multi-party elections in Albania

July 1991 Warsaw Pact dissolved

March 1992 Opposition Democratic Party wins Albanian elections

THE BREAKUP OF YUGOSLAVIA

Under Tito, Yugoslavia appeared to be a happily united multi-ethnic nation. After his death, however, old antagonisms returned, and the country soon broke apart.

AFTER TITO

Tito was a Croat but was accepted by the Serbs, Slovenes, and other Yugoslavs because he was a strong, unifying leader. He was concerned, however, that he had no successor who could hold the nation together. In 1974, he introduced a new constitution that set up an eight-person collective presidency to govern the country after his death. One president was to come from each of the six Yugoslav republics, and one each was to come from the mainly Albanian province of Kosovo and the mainly Hungarian province of Vojvodina. Each president would hold power for one year, with all eight choosing a prime minister once every four years.

At first, the system worked well, and an orderly transition of power took place as planned. But economic problems forced the entire government to resign in 1988. From then on, the individual republics increasingly ran their own economic and political affairs. Slovenia and Croatia elected non-communist governments, while Serbia became increasingly nationalist.

> ### *"Srbija je ustala" ("Serbia has arisen")*
>
> **Serbian political chant, 1989**

MILOSEVIC

In 1987, Slobodan Milosevic (1941-) took power in Serbia. Two years later, he removed autonomous status from Kosovo and

Vojvodina, giving Serbia four votes (including that of its ally, Montenegro) in the collective presidency. This forced the four other republics—Slovenia, Croatia, Bosnia, and Macedonia—to work together to stop Serbia.

The Slovene president stated that Milosevic had turned "Yugoslavia into Serbo-slavia." No one wanted to preserve Yugoslavia, and in 1991, the central government completely broke

MILOSEVIC'S RISE TO POWER

Born in northeast Serbia, Slobodan Milosevic made the Serb capital, Belgrade, his power base. He became leader of the Serbia Communist Party in 1987 and president of Serbia two years later. He stirred up Serb hostility toward Hungarian and Albanian minorities and campaigned for a Greater Serbia to unite Serbs under Serbian rule. This alarmed the other five republics and was the main cause of the eventual breakup of Yugoslavia during the 1990s.

A Croatian soldier walks past a wrecked car in a Serb village during the fighting in 1995.

down. All power was now in the hands of the six republics. Milosevic refused to accept a Croat as republican president, for he wanted to dominate Yugoslavia himself. Croatia and Slovenia then proclaimed their independence from Yugoslavia, followed by Macedonia. Federal Yugoslav (largely Serb) troops attacked Slovenia, but peace was declared in a week. Fighting with Croatia lasted until January 1992, and when the Yugoslav army withdrew, it left a large Serb force in eastern Croatia. Croatia recovered control of this in 1998, but by then, Yugoslavia had collapsed.

ETHNIC DIVISIONS IN YUGOSLAVIA, 1991

SLOVENIA
CROATIA
VOJVODINA
BOSNIA-HERZEGOVINA
SERBIA
MONTE-NEGRO
KOSOVO
MACEDONIA

- Serbs
- Hungarians
- Albanians
- Muslims
- Croats
- Slovenes
- Macedonians

THE COLLAPSE OF YUGOSLAVIA

May 1974 Tito elected president for life, with rotating eight-person presidency to run the country after his death

May 1980 Tito dies

1987 Slobodan Milosevic becomes leader of Serbian Communist Party

1988 Yugoslav economy collapses; nationalist

demonstrations in Serbia and Montenegro

December 1988 Yugoslav government resigns when parliament rejects reforms

March 1989 Milosevic ends autonomy of Kosovo and Vojvodina

May 1989 Milosevic becomes president of Serbia

March 1991 Yugoslav government breaks down completely

May 1991 Serbia refuses to accept a Croat, Stipe Mesic, as Yugoslav president

June 1991 Slovenia and Croatia declare independence

July 1991 European Community imposes

truce in Slovenia

September 1991 Macedonia declares independence

January 1992 Yugoslav (Serb) forces withdraw from most of Croatia

November 1995 Croatia recovers territory from Serb forces

BOSNIA

The breakup of Yugoslavia hit Bosnia the hardest, and it became the battleground for the worst fighting in Europe since World War II.

THE ROAD TO INDEPENDENCE

The republic of Bosnia-Herzegovina was always the most multi-ethnic (mixed) part of Yugoslavia. Its population was roughly 44 percent Muslim, 31 percent Serb, 17 percent Croat, and 8 percent other groups. Intermarriage was common, intercommunal conflict was rare, and different religions and cultures were respected.

But when Croatia and Slovenia declared their independence, Bosnia's future became bleak. In March 1991, the Serb and Croat leaders agreed to divide Bosnia between them. After the end of the Croatian war in January 1992, Bosnia feared that it might be attacked next and declared its independence.

> ### The leaders of Yugoslavia "were stirring a cauldron of blood that would soon boil over."
>
> **Misha Glenny, BBC journalist and historian, February 1991**

BITTER CONFLICT

Bosnian Serbs immediately rejected this declaration and set up an independent Republika Srpska in eastern Bosnia. A three-way war then broke out, with Muslims defending themselves against both Croat and Serb forces, while elsewhere an uneasy coalition of Muslims and Croats fought the Serbs. By 1993, Serbs held 70 percent of Bosnia but were not strong enough to conquer the rest.

Attempts to end the conflict were only partly successful. The UN imposed sanctions against Serbia, set up a Muslim-Croat federation in Herzegovina, and established six Muslim "safe areas." But NATO air strikes failed to deter the Bosnian Serbs, who overran the areas in 1995, killing thousands of unarmed Muslims.

A NATO air strike destroys a Serb ammunition depot in 1995.

36

THE BOSNIAN WAR

The Bosnian Serbs were armed with weapons, tanks, and "volunteers" supplied by Serbia. They expelled or killed all non-Serbs through a policy of "ethnic cleansing." Serb troops bombarded the Bosnian capital, Sarajevo, and overran Muslim towns and villages, sending the inhabitants into detention camps. Croat troops challenged Muslims in the southern town of Mostar, capital of Herzegovina, and reduced the historic city to ruins. Both Serbs and Croats committed appalling crimes. By the end of the war in 1995, at least 250,000 had died, including one in three Muslims. Thousands were homeless and many more were refugees.

Mostar's famous 16th-century bridge in ruins, 1993.

PEACE

In August 1995, Croatia expelled the Serb forces occupying its Krajina region and invaded Serb regions of Bosnia. Serb morale collapsed when NATO planes bombarded Serb positions around Sarajevo, while support from Serbia itself dried up as sanctions began to bite. A peace deal was finally agreed on between the presidents of Serbia, Croatia, and Bosnia at Dayton, Ohio. The agreement set up two separate states within Bosnia: the Muslim-Croat Federation occupied 51 percent of the country, Republika Srpska the rest. The war was over, and Bosnia had just survived.

Croat-Muslim Federation

Republika Srpska

BOSNIA AFTER THE DAYTON AGREEMENT

THE BOSNIAN WAR

March 24, 1991 Milosevic and the Croat leader Franjo Tudjman agree to divide Bosnia between them

January 1992 Yugoslav (Serb) forces end war against Croatia

February 1992 Bosnians vote in a referendum for independence from Yugoslavia

March 1992 Bosnia declares independence; Serbs set up independent republic

May 1992 UN imposes economic and military sanctions on Serbia

June 1992 UN intervenes for first time in Bosnia by taking over Sarajevo airport to fly in relief supplies

August 1992 UN condemns "ethnic cleansing" by Serbs and approves the use of force to restore peace

May 1993 UN establishes "safe havens" for Muslims

March 1994 Muslims and Croats form federation in Herzegovina

April 1994 NATO begins air strikes against Bosnian Serb positions

July 1995 Bosnian Serb troops murder 8,000 Muslims in Srebrenica

August 1995 Croatian attack on Serb-held territory in Krajina

November 1995 Dayton peace accord ends war

KOSOVO

With the independence of Croatia, Slovenia, Macedonia, and, by 1995, Bosnia, Yugoslavia was reduced to just Serbia and Montenegro. The final breakup of the country caused even more bloodshed.

Slobodan Milosevic addresses Serbs at Kosovo Polje, June 28, 1989.

THE IMPORTANCE OF KOSOVO

The southern Serbian province of Kosovo is inhabited largely by Kosovo Albanians; in 1992, Serbs and others made up only 18 percent of the total population. But the region has great historical importance for Serbia. On June 28, 1389, the Ottoman Turks defeated the Serbs at the Battle of Kosovo Polje, ending Serbian independence for almost 500 years. The battle site itself did not become part of Serbia again until 1913.

Under the terms of the 1946 Yugoslav constitution, Kosovo became an autonomous province within Serbia. It gained more powers in the years that followed. When Milosevic came to power in Serbia, however, he reversed this policy. In 1989, just before the 600th anniversary of the battle, Milosevic ended Kosovo's autonomy and sent in troops to suppress dissent. At celebrations to mark the battle, he warned of future wars in the region.

> *"Six centuries [after the Battle of Kosovo], we are again engaged in battles and quarrels. They are not armed battles, but this cannot be excluded."*
>
> **Slobodan Milosevic at Kosovo Polje, June 28, 1989**

CONFLICT

Throughout the 1990s, Kosovo Albanian resentment against Serbia rose, particularly when the Serbs who had been displaced from Croatia in 1995 were resettled in Kosovo. The Kosovo Liberation Army (KLA) was formed by Kosovo Albanians to protect their interests and confronted Serb troops for the first time in 1998. During that year, fighting intensified, as the Serbs attacked villages and massacred their inhabitants.

In 1998-99, peace talks in Paris proposed full autonomy for Kosovo, with the possibility of a referendum on full independence after three or five years. Serbia refused to accept this settlement, so NATO bombers attacked the country in an 11-week campaign. The Serbian capital, Belgrade, was bombed, and its bridges were destroyed.

The Serbs responded with a renewed policy of ethnic cleansing by forcing 600,000 Kosovo Albanians to flee their homes and seek safety in Albania or Macedonia. Milosevic eventually capitulated and Serb troops left the province to be replaced by 40,000 NATO peacekeepers under a UN interim administration. The fighting was over.

MACEDONIA

The southern Yugoslav republic of Macedonia broke peacefully from Yugoslavia in 1991. But Greece challenged its right to independence, because it feared that Macedonia had territorial ambitions in northern Greece (once part of the historic Macedonia). Greece persuaded the EU to withhold recognition until 1993, when the new state became known as the Former Yugoslav Republic of Macedonia. Greece continued calling the new state the Skopje Republic after its capital city. Many Kosovo Albanian refugees fled there, increasing the tense relationships in the country between Macedonians and Albanians.

Fleeing for his life, a young Kosovo Albanian refugee pushes packages of humanitarian aid in a wheelbarrow, 1998.

THE END OF YUGOSLAVIA

January 1946 Macedonia becomes one of six republics within Yugoslavia; Kosovo becomes an autonomous province of Serbia

1987 Milosevic comes to power in Serbia

March 1989 Milosevic ends autonomy of Kosovo within Serbia

June 1989 Milosevic whips up Serb nationalist feelings at the 600th anniversary celebrations of the Battle of Kosovo Polje

September 1991 Macedonia declares independence

December 1993 EU grants recognition to the "Former Yugoslav Republic of Macedonia"

October 1995 Greeks lift trade embargo on Macedonia

1997 Foundation of KLA

January 1998 First clashes between KLA and Serb troops

1998–99 Abortive peace talks at Paris, France, fail to settle Kosovo crisis

March 1999 NATO planes begin 11-week bombing campaign against Serbia; ethnic cleansing sends 600,000 Kosovo Albanians into exile

June 1999 Milosevic accepts peace in Kosovo

July 1999 NATO troops take over Kosovo

The Balkans may sometimes seem a remote and violent place, far from Europe. But the Balkans are as much a part of Europe as Britain. Today, a fragile peace exists, but many issues remain unresolved and could lead to further conflict.

INTEGRATION

The two main organizations that have bound Europe together since World War II are the North Atlantic Treaty Organization (NATO) and the European Union (EU). Both are pro-western and do not allow communist states as members, so all the Balkan states (except Greece) were once excluded from them. Greece has been a member of NATO since 1952 and of the EU since 1981, adopting the euro (money used in the EU) in 2002.

Slovenia joined both organizations in 2004. Bulgaria and Romania also joined NATO in 2004, and both have applied for EU membership—although they are unlikely to be admitted until 2007. These countries are now democracies, although both Romania and Bulgaria remain very poor. Relations between Greece and Turkey (over Cyprus) and Macedonia (over its name) remain tense. Romania's treatment of its minority Hungarian population causes difficulties with Hungary.

SEPARATION

Albania and the former Yugoslavia, apart from Slovenia, still remain separate from the rest of Europe. Albania is desperately poor and unstable and needs substantial foreign assistance to overcome its many economic and social problems. Croatia is still recovering from its lengthy war with Serbia, and the once ethnically mixed country is now almost completely Croat. Only four percent of the population is

Serb, because more than 150,000 Serbs fled Croatia in 1995. In the last few years, Croatia has begun to integrate with the rest of Europe, and tourists are starting to return to its beautiful Adriatic coastline.

Tourism in Croatia is beginning to recover from the ravages of the wars of the 1990s.

Bosnia is still recovering from war, and an international tribunal is trying people suspected of war crimes. This includes Slobodan Milosevic, the former leader of Serbia. Serbia is now trying to establish peaceful relations with all its neighbors.

Kosovo's future is still in doubt. Will it reintegrate with Serbia, become independent, or merge with Albania? The answer may partly depend on how long NATO wants to keep its troops in the country.

The rights of Albanians are also an issue in Macedonia, where many refugees fled from Kosovo in 1999 to join the half a million Albanians already there (25 percent of the total population). Violence between

An ethnic Albanian family lives in a tent beside the ruins of their Kosovo home in 1999.

Macedonians and Albanians flared in 2001, and a NATO force was sent to the country to restore order. A new constitution is meant to reconcile the two communities, but tensions remain high.

THE FUTURE

Serbs, Croats, and Slovenes now live peacefully in the northern Balkans, but relations between Kosovo Albanians, Macedonians, and Serbs continue to cause problems in the south. As long as these issues remain unresolved and borders remain in dispute, this region will continue to be one of the most potentially dangerous flashpoints in Europe.

THE BALKANS TODAY

November 1993 UN International Criminal Tribunal for the Former Yugoslavia opens at The Hague, in the Netherlands

May 1999 Slobodan Milosevic charged with war crimes

September 2000

Milosevic defeated in first round of Yugoslav presidential election

April 2001 Milosevic arrested for war crimes and in June is sent to The Hague for trial

January 2002 Greece adopts the euro as currency

March 2002 Yugoslavia dissolved; Serbia and Montenegro form loose confederation

March–September 2002 Violent conflict in Macedonia with the militant Albanian National Liberation Army (NLA) ended by NATO intervention;

NLA is disarmed and a new constitution agreed on to protect Albanian rights

September 2003 Renewed clashes in Macedonia with NLA

May 2004 Slovenia joins EU and NATO; Romania and Bulgaria join NATO

GLOSSARY

Annex To formally take over a neighboring country or province.

Assassination Murder of a public or political figure, usually by a surprise attack.

Autonomous Semi-independent part of a country with considerable powers of self-government.

Comecon Council for Mutual Economic Assistance, a Soviet-led economic organization set up in 1949. It linked all the communist economies of the Balkans and eastern Europe (except Yugoslavia) with the USSR.

Communism Belief in a society without different social classes in which everyone is equal and where all property is owned by the people.

Constitution Written document setting out principles on which a country is founded and the rights its people enjoy.

Coup, or *coup d'état* Sudden violent or illegal overthrow of an existing government.

Democracy Government by the people or their elected representatives.

Dictator Unelected head of state or government who rules a country by force.

Empire Group of peoples or countries governed by one ruler.

Ethnic cleansing Deliberate policy of forcibly removing ethnic groups from an area in order to make it ethnically pure.

European Union Union of 25 European nations with common currency, trade, and other links.

Fascism Right-wing political movement based on authority, often military, and nationalism, which stresses the power of the state over the individual.

Guerrilla Member of an unofficial, usually politically motivated, armed force.

Iron Curtain Phrase used by Winston Churchill in 1946 to describe the military, political, and economic division of Europe into a Soviet-dominated communist east, including the Balkans, and an American-dominated capitalist west.

Migration Mass movement of people from one country or region to another.

Minority Group of people who form a distinct but small group within a nation and who are different from the majority of the population.

Monarchy Country ruled by a hereditary king or queen.

Nationalist Person who is loyal or passionately devoted to his or her own country.

NATO North Atlantic Treaty Organization, a defense organization including the U.S. and most western European states.

Nazi Party Extreme fascist party of Adolf Hitler that ruled Germany from 1933-45.

Pagan Person without any religion, or who is not Christian, Jewish, or Muslim.

Parliamentary government Government by elected representatives of the people.

Partisan Member of an armed resistance group fighting inside a country against an invading or occupying army.

Peninsula Strip of land projecting out into the sea or seas from the mainland.

Power Nation that has great influence over international affairs.

Red Army The army of the Soviet Union.

Refugee Person who has fled from danger in one country to seek refuge in another, safer country.

Republic Country governed by an elected head of state called a president.

Right-wing Political views that stress authority, strong government, and a belief in existing institutions; the opposite of left-wing political views.

Royalist Person who believes in government by monarchy with a king or queen as head of state.

Sanctions Diplomatic, military, economic, and other measures established by the UN against a member nation that has violated international law or failed to act on a UN resolution.

Sultan Muslim ruler of the Ottoman Empire.

United Nations (UN) An international peacekeeping organization, founded in 1945 and based in New York.

USSR Union of the Soviet Socialist Republics, or the Soviet Union, which existed from 1922-91; commonly known as Soviet Russia.

Warsaw Pact Soviet-led military pact, set up in 1955, establishing a unified military command linking all the communist states of the Balkans and eastern Europe (except Yugoslavia) with the USSR.

INDEX

A

Albania 9, 18-20, 23-25, 28-30, 32-34, 38-41
Allies 20, 21
Austria 14-15, 17, 28
Austria-Hungary 18-22

B

Balkans
  communism in 26-29, 32, 33
  geography 8-9
  history 10-13
  postwar 22, 23
  Wars 19, 20
Bosnia-Herzegovina 9, 11, 17-20, 22, 24, 25, 28, 34, 38, 41
  War 36, 37
Britain 15, 17, 20, 25, 30, 31, 40
Bulgaria 8, 9, 11-13, 16-27, 29, 30, 33, 40, 41
Byzantine Empire 8, 10-13

C

Ceausescu, N. 27, 33
Central Powers 20, 21
Chetnik 24, 25, 28
Christianity 9-11, 13, 14, 43
Churchill, W. 26, 27, 30, 31, 42
communism 26-30, 32-35, 42
Congress of Berlin 16, 17
Constantinople 8, 10-17, 19, 21
Croatia 9, 11, 14, 15, 22, 24, 28, 34-40
Cyprus 17, 30, 40

D

Dimitrov, G. 26

E

East Rumelia 17
European Union (EU) 31, 39-42

F

Ferdinand, Archduke F. 20, 21
fighters, resistance 24, 25
France 15, 17, 20, 25

G

Germany 20, 21, 24-27, 30, 31, 43
Gorbachev, M. 32, 33
Greece 9-11, 15, 17-25, 27, 30, 31, 39, 40

H

Hitler, A. 24, 43
Hoxha, E. 28, 29, 32
Hungary 9, 13-15, 22, 24, 26, 33, 34, 40

I

Islam 12, 13
Italy 18, 19, 24, 25, 27, 29, 32

J

Jews 9, 13, 18, 24, 25, 43

K

Kingdom of the Serbs 23
Kosovo 9, 29, 34, 35, 38, 39, 41
Kosovo Liberation Army (KLA) 39

M

Macedonia 9, 11, 16-19, 26, 28, 34, 35, 38-41
Michael, King 26, 27
Milosevic, S. 34, 35, 38, 39, 41
Montenegro 9, 16, 18-22, 25, 28, 34, 38, 41
Muslim 9, 12-15, 18, 24, 36, 37, 43
Mussolini, B. 24

N

National Socialist (Nazi) Party 24, 30, 31, 43
North Atlantic Treaty Organization (NATO) 36, 37, 39-41, 43

O

Orthodox Church 9, 11, 13, 14, 18
Ottoman Empire 8, 12-17, 20-23, 38, 43
  end of 18-20

R

Red Army 25-27, 32, 43
refugee 22, 23, 37, 39, 41, 43
Roman Catholic Church 9, 11, 13, 18
Roman Empire 8, 10, 11, 24
Romania 9, 11, 14-17, 19, 20-27, 29, 33, 40, 41
Russia 10, 11, 13-18, 20, 22, 26, 43 see also USSR

S

San Stefano, Treaty of 16, 17, 18
Serbia 9, 11-16, 18-22, 25, 28, 29, 34-41
Slavs 10, 11, 16, 20, 22
Slovenia 9, 22, 28, 34-36, 38, 40, 41
Soviet Union see Russia
Stalin, J. 26-31

T

Tito, J. B. 25, 28-30, 34, 35
Transylvania 14, 15, 22, 23
Turkey 8, 9, 12, 13, 15, 22, 23, 30, 40

U

Union of the Soviet Socialist Republics (USSR) 24, 25, 27-29, 32, 33, 42, 43
United Nations (UN) 32, 36, 37, 41, 43
United States (U.S.) 26, 27, 30-32, 43

V

Vojvodim 34, 35, 39

W

World War I 8, 20, 21, 22
World War II 24-25, 30, 36, 40

Y

Yugoslavia 9, 22-30, 34-43